I0766375

HOBBIES
TO
MAKE MONEY
Sometimes

JOYCE SHEARIN

Trafford
PUBLISHING

1.   Pillow pictures for decoration.

2.   Karaoke tape songs

3. At home business within the hour local delivery of items.

4. Jewelry/bead making/stringy

5.   Prepare taxes.

6.   Write profession books with
      certificate of graduation in
      back.

7.   Do construction-home fix up/
      new home build.

8.   Do car maintenance/mechanic.

9. Start a basketball, golf, new sports team.

10. Create an electronic golf game.

11. Start a black (fair priced)
    by mail and internet based
    private/public school. (that can
    be paid by the government)
    (due to too many problems in
    schools now with education,
    equity, cost, discriminate, etc.)

12. Write good poetry-plaques,
    frames (for motivation, etc.)

13. Start a record concert town
     group.

14. Cellphone provider affordable.

15. Open a music store that also develops good music artists live up top or in back also to monitor good.

16. Crochet/Knit; gloves, hats, scarves, beenies, (head fashion coverings.)

17. Films (make good short legal) about issues, lives, good ideas, etc. to show on cable, TV, donation showings, events, dance arena breaks, sports breaks, etc.

18. Make a talent school or class in a book.

19. Do home construction affordable with land included build, on nice good safe valuable places.

20. Security escort contractor.

23. Crochet Scarfs *Check for internet a friend sometimes tips and donations

24. Make gloves leather knit fabric etc.

25. Hold dace class *Catering from cooking for good.

26. Hold a hip hop exercise meeting group.

27. Assist as needed a relative or
    friend.

28. Do nails.

29. Open a music store R & B/Hip
     Hop Thank you.

30. Make Spaghetti, bowls.

31.   Make dilled cucumbers. (Add vinegar)

32.   Barber Hairstylist on call.

33. Make clothes.

34. Open a Pharmacy

About the Author

The author is a military veteran and has a doctor of arts degree. She is also a Minister, Educated graduate, and Law School Graduate Awarded.

www.ingramcontent.com/pod-product-compliance
Lightning Source LLC
Chambersburg PA
CBHW051423250726
48655CB00003B/1201